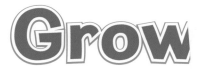

Grow

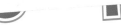

By Erica Bland

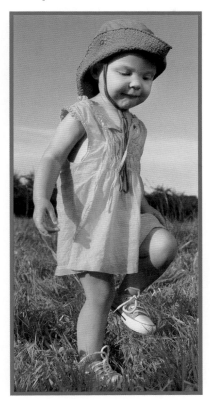

Scott Foresman
is an imprint of

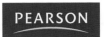

Glenview, Illinois • Boston, Massachusetts • Chandler, Arizona •
Upper Saddle River, New Jersey

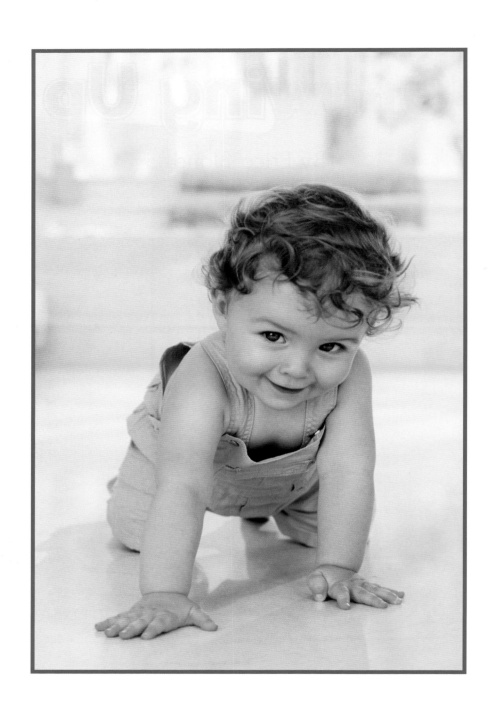

I can crawl.

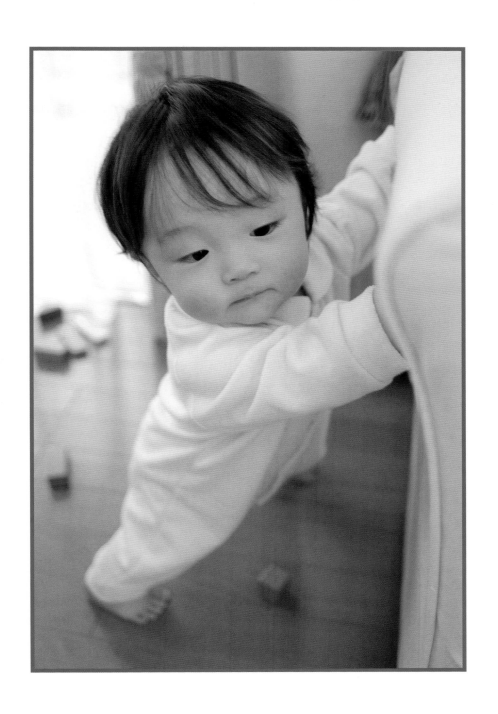

I can stand.

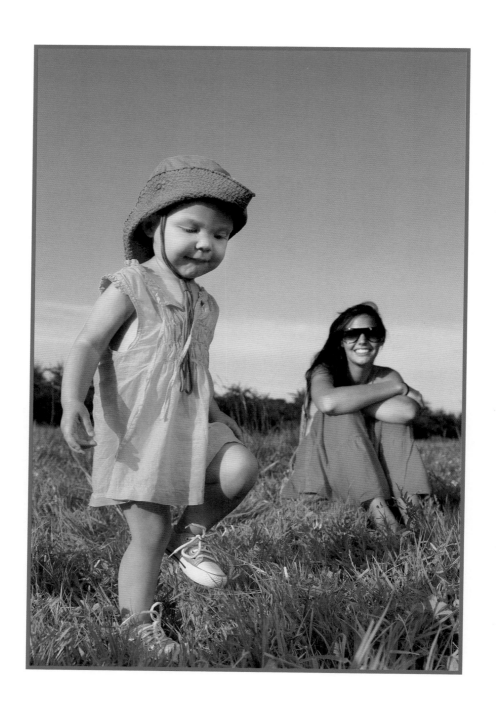

I can walk.

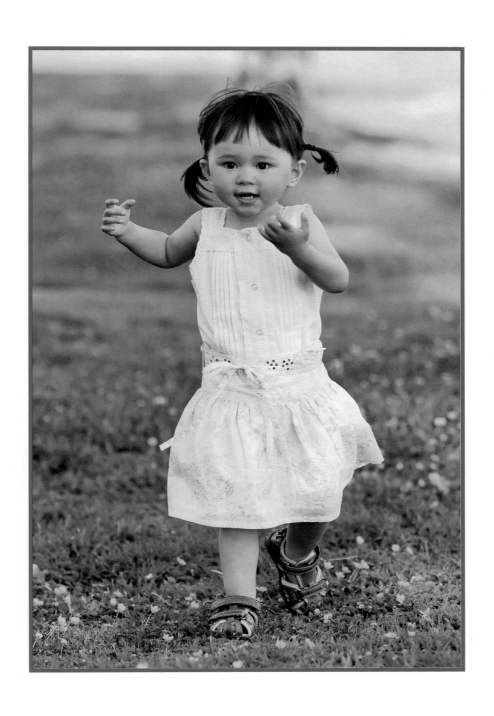

I can run.

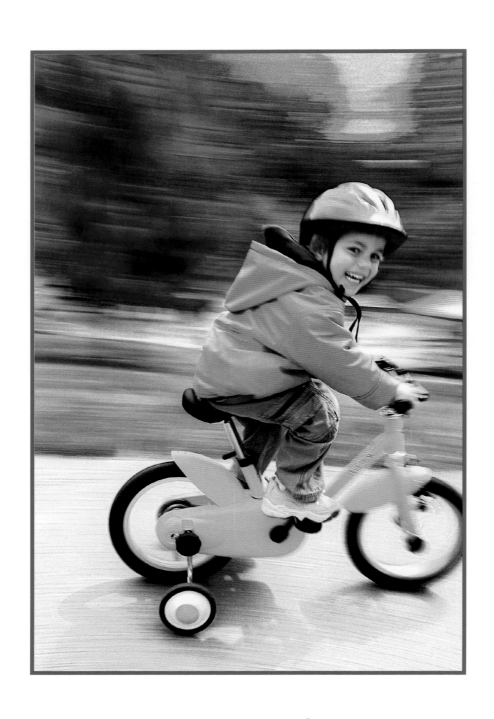

I can ride.

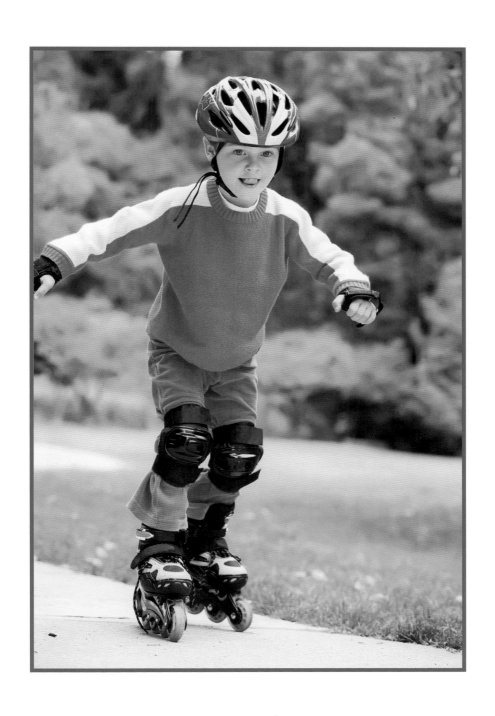

I can skate.

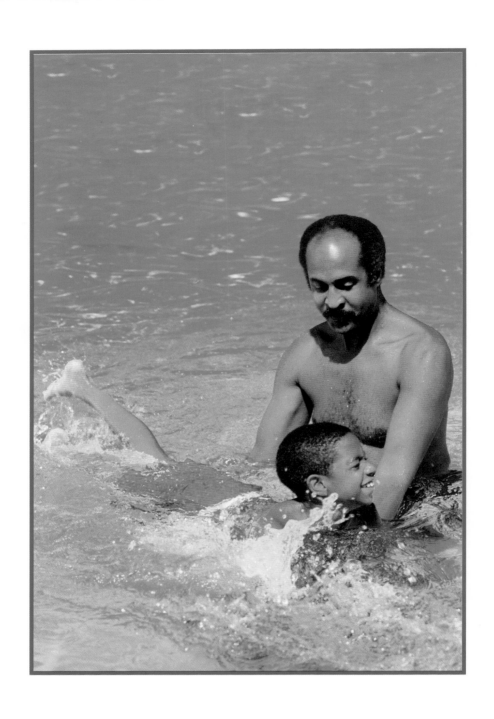

I can swim.